UNUSUAL FARM ANIMALS

RAISING BEES

THERESA EMMINIZER

I0808967

PowerKiDS press.
New York

Published in 2020 by The Rosen Publishing Group, Inc.
29 East 21st Street, New York, NY 10010

Copyright © 2020 by The Rosen Publishing Group, Inc.

All rights reserved. No part of this book may be reproduced in any form without permission in writing from the publisher, except by a reviewer.

First Edition

Editor: Tanya Dellaccio
Book Design: Michael Flynn

Photo Credits: Cover (bees) weter78/Shutterstock.com; (series barn wood background) PASAKORN RANGSIYANONT/Shutterstock.com; (series wood frame) robert_s/Shutterstock.com; cover, pp. 1, 3, 23, 24 (bee icon) Denis_M/Shutterstock.com; p. 5 Valentina Zhi/Shutterstock.com; p. 6 DEA/G. LOVERA/De Agostini Editorial/Getty Images; p. 7 Album/Alamy; p. 9 Nitr/Shutterstock.com; p. 11 Lehrer/Shutterstock.com; p. 12 NoPainNoGain/Shutterstock.com; p. 13 sergey kolesnikov/Shutterstock.com; p. 15 (main) Rudmer Zwerver/Shutterstock.com; p. 15 (inset) Natalie Board/Shutterstock.com; p. 17 santypan/Shutterstock.com; p. 18 Lindsay Snow/Shutterstock.com; p. 19 Sushaaa/Shutterstock.com; p. 21 Darios/Shutterstock.com; p. 22 Daniel Prudek/Shutterstock.com.

Library of Congress Cataloging-in-Publication Data

Names: Emminizer, Theresa, author.
Title: Raising bees / Theresa Emminizer.
Other titles: Unusual farm animals.
Description: New York : PowerKids Press, [2020] | Series: Unusual farm animals | Includes index.
Identifiers: LCCN 2019017698| ISBN 9781725308862 (pbk.) | ISBN 9781725308886 (library bound) | ISBN 9781725308879 (6 pack)
Subjects: LCSH: Honeybee–Juvenile literature. | Bee culture–Juvenile literature.
Classification: LCC SF523.5 .E46 2020 | DDC 638/.1–dc23
LC record available at https://lccn.loc.gov/2019017698

Manufactured in the United States of America

CPSIA Compliance Information: Batch #CWPK20. For Further Information contact Rosen Publishing, New York, New York at 1-800-237-9932.

CONTENTS

THE BUZZ ABOUT BEES

When you think of livestock, or farm animals raised for **profit** or other uses, you probably picture cows, chickens, or pigs. But did you know that bees can be livestock, too?

Honeybees collect nectar from flowers, turn it partly into honey, and store it in honeycombs. Over time, it turns fully into honey. Bees store honey to eat in the winter when they can't gather nectar or pollen from flowers. People have been keeping bees and collecting their honey for thousands of years.

HOW UNUSUAL!

There are over 20,000 types of bees. Bumblebees and honeybees are the most commonly known. Unlike bumblebees, honeybees are often raised in farm-like settings.

A PLACE WHERE PEOPLE KEEP HONEYBEES IS CALLED AN APIARY.

BEEKEEPING THROUGH HISTORY

People have **harvested** honey for at least 8,000 years, but beekeeping, or owning bees for honey or profit, began later. Beekeeping existed as far back as 2500 BC in ancient Egypt.

PAINTING FROM 500 BC IN THE TOMB OF PASABA, EGYPT

COLLECTING HONEY IS SOMETIMES CALLED "HONEY HUNTING." THIS CAVE PAINTING FOUND NEAR VALENCIA, SPAIN, SHOWS A HONEY HUNTER. IT WAS MADE AROUND 8,000 YEARS AGO!

Ancient Egyptians created man-made beehives out of clay or baskets covered in mud. Some apiaries held as many as 500 beehives! The Egyptians collected honey by blowing smoke into the hives. This sent the bees out of the hive so that people could reach in and collect the honey without being stung.

BENEFITS OF BEEKEEPING

There are many reasons to raise honeybees. Honey and wax, which are made by bees, have many uses. Honey is tasty to eat, eases sore throats, and has many health benefits. It can even be used to help heal burns! People also use honey in beauty products such as shampoos and use wax in candles and **balms**.

Bees also keep plants healthy through **pollination**. Pollination boosts plant and fruit growth. A farmer or gardener can make their crops healthier just by keeping bees!

HOW UNUSUAL!

Honeybees pollinate around 80 percent of the crops grown in the United States. There are around 2.4 million honeybee colonies in the United States today.

HONEY IS SO USEFUL THAT IT'S SOMETIMES CALLED LIQUID GOLD!

INSIDE THE HIVE

Honeybees live in groups called hives or colonies. There are three types of bees in a colony: the queen, workers, and drones. The queen bee is the most important member of the colony. She lays all the eggs. A queen bee can lay up to 2,500 eggs in a single day.

Other female bees are called workers. Their job is to build and **protect** the hive and to collect pollen and nectar. Male bees are called drones. Their job is to **mate** with the queen bee.

HOW UNUSUAL!

Bees can dance! Worker bees show each other where to find the best food by moving in a pattern called the "waggle dance."

THE QUEEN BEE IS THE LARGEST BEE IN THE COLONY. SHE MEASURES ABOUT 0.8 TO 0.9 INCH (20 TO 23 MM) LONG. WORKERS ARE 0.4 TO 0.7 INCH (11 TO 17 MM) LONG AND DRONES ARE 0.55 TO 0.6 INCH (14 TO 16 MM) LONG.
WORKER BEE
QUEEN BEE

A BEE'S LIFE

Honeybees grow in four stages: egg to larva to pupa to adult. The queen drops eggs into cells in the hive built by worker bees. After three days, the eggs **hatch** into larvae. The larvae eat and grow. Soon, the worker bees seal the larvae inside the cells with wax.

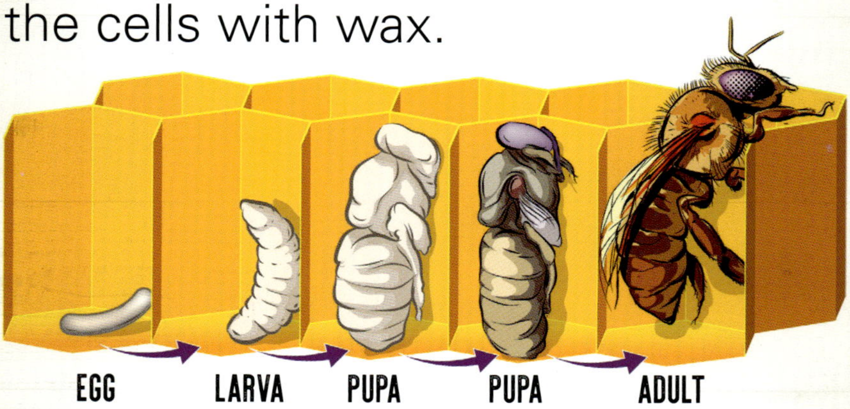

HOW UNUSUAL!

Queen honeybees live up to five years. When the queen bee dies, the colony chooses a young larva to be the new queen. They feed it a special food called royal jelly.

IT'S BELIEVED THAT BEES MAKE THEIR HONEYCOMBS HEXAGONS, OR SHAPES WITH 6 SIDES, BECAUSE THEY FIT TOGETHER ALMOST PERFECTLY.

Inside each cell, a larva spins a cocoon and becomes a pupa. Inside the cocoon, the pupa's legs, wings, and eyes develop. When it's fully grown, it eats its way out of the wax cell as an adult bee.

CHOOSING YOUR HIVE

Beekeepers use many different kinds of hives. Two of the most popular styles of modern beehives in the United States are the Langstroth hive and the top-bar hive. Both kinds are usually made of wood.

Langstroth hives are square boxes that are stacked on top of one another. The upper boxes hold wooden frames, which the bees fill with honey and honeycombs. Top-bar hives are **trough**-shaped, with a removable cover. There are no frames in a top-bar hive. Instead, the bees build the combs on wooden bars.

HOW UNUSUAL!

The Reverend Lorenzo Langstroth, a beekeeper from Philadelphia, Pennsylvania, created the Langstroth style of hive in 1851. It's still the most common beekeeping system in the United States.

LANGSTROTH HIVES ARE OFTEN USED IN LARGE-SCALE APIARIES, WHILE TOP-BAR HIVES ARE POPULAR WITH SMALLER BACKYARD BEEKEEPERS.

TOOLS OF THE TRADE

You only need a few small tools to keep bees. A bee smoker is a metal can with handles that help blow air into the can. The beekeeper builds a small fire at the bottom of the can and pumps the handles to fan the fire and release smoke. The smoke both confuses and calms the bees.

Beekeepers use hive tools to pull apart the boxes that make up the beehive. They use scrapers to remove wax. They also use uncapping scratchers to open the honeycomb to get the honey.

HOW UNUSUAL!

Honeybees are fast! They fly about 15.5 miles (25 km) per hour. Their wings can flap 200 times every second.

BEEKEEPERS ALSO NEED PROTECTIVE CLOTHING. BEE SUITS, GLOVES, AND HATS WITH VEILS HELP KEEP THEM FROM BEING STUNG. IT'S IMPORTANT FOR BEEKEEPERS TO STAY CALM SO THAT THEY DON'T UPSET THE BEES.

BEEKEEPING BASICS

The most important part of beekeeping is the honeybee itself! Bees are small and **fragile**, and they need to be cared for gently.

BEES CAN BE ORDERED ONLINE OR BOUGHT FROM LOCAL SUPPLIERS.

Bees' basic needs include water, pollen, and nectar. They also need protection from the cold, wind, and rain. They need privacy, too. Hives should be in a quiet, protected area that isn't too close to noisy cars or people. They need to be kept dry and off the ground so that bugs can't crawl inside. It's also important to make sure the bees are close to fresh water.

CHALLENGES OF BEEKEEPING

Bee colonies need at least 50 to 60 pounds (22 to 27 kg) of stored honey to live through the winter. Beekeepers must make sure their bees have enough food in the spring to create the honey they'll eat during winter.

If there isn't enough nectar around for bees to collect in nature, beekeepers can feed them a combination of sugar and water. Bees can also be fed sugar candy or pollen patties. Bees should never be fed store-bought honey, as it can make them sick.

HOW UNUSUAL!

Bees can die if they aren't kept warm enough. The hive should never be opened unless the temperature is above 40°F (4.4°C) with no wind.

THIS BEEKEEPER IS POURING SUGAR SYRUP INTO A FEEDER FOR HIS BEES.

THE FUTURE OF BEES

Bees play a key role, or part, in the health of our **environment**. They help flowers and plants grow and make **habitats** better for other insects and animals. They are an important part of the food chain, affecting many other animals. People need bees to pollinate the crops that we eat.

Pesticides, habitat changes, and sicknesses can put bees in danger. This can lead to colony collapse disorder, or CCD, which is the disappearance of worker bees. Today, beekeeping has become more important than ever before.

GLOSSARY

balm: An ointment, or cream, to heal skin.

environment: The natural world around us.

fragile: Easily broken or hurt.

habitat: The natural home for plants, animals, and other living things.

harvest: To gather.

hatch: To break open or come out of.

mate: To come together to make babies.

nectar: A sweet liquid produced by plants and used by bees in making honey.

pesticide: Poisons used to kill pests.

pollination: Taking pollen from one flower, plant, or tree to another.

profit: Money that is made.

protect: To keep safe.

trough: A long, narrow container.

INDEX

WEBSITES

Due to the changing nature of Internet links, PowerKids Press has developed an online list of websites related to the subject of this book. This site is updated regularly. Please use this link to access the list: www.powerkidslinks.com/ufa/bees